Throw
Away
the
Garbage

THROW
AWAY
THE
GARBAGE

Buckner Fanning

WORD BOOKS, PUBLISHER • Waco, Texas

to Martha
whose radiant life and inspiring love
constantly brighten all my days

"Reckless Pink,"
"Intoxication,"
and the
"Ten Commandments"

IT IS ALWAYS wonderfully refreshing and exciting to see truth come to life and walk around in everyday clothes. This seems to happen most often with the young, which just reaffirms the fact that "a child shall lead them." I have often been led and taught by my children, and one particular incident stands out dramatically in my mind.

Some years ago when our sons Michael and Stephen were about nine and six years of age, I gave them each a couple of dollars to buy their Mother's Day gifts. I thought this was a stroke of genius on my part which would help them feel they actually had a part in the selection of their gifts to Martha. On the Saturday prior to Mother's Day the three of us drove to our local drugstore where I released Mike and Steve, each firmly clutching two dollars.

Watching them, I couldn't believe my eyes! They stormed into that drugstore like the Marines landing on Iwo Jima. It was a terrifying thing to witness. In self-defense I quickly found the soda fountain and tried to hide. Sitting there, casually pretending to drink a cup of coffee, I would occasionally glimpse some unsuspecting shopper frantically seeking refuge from the confusion being created by my two commandoes in search of gifts. Every few moments I would hear Mike or Steve yell at the top of his voice, "Come see what I've found." To say I will never forget that day is a gross understatement. A citizen of San Francisco in 1906 would forget the earthquake sooner than I will forget that Saturday.

Nine-year-old Michael had been watching some lipstick commercials on television, and so he finally landed at the lipstick display. After uncapping nearly every tube in a large tray, which nearly drove the saleslady up the wall, he finally decided on a shade. I wish you could have seen that lipstick. For that matter, it was so loud I wish you could have heard it. It was iridescent; the "thing" glowed in the dark. If Martha ever wore it, you could see her coming three blocks away. They could have used that lipstick at the airport on foggy nights to light the runways. But since it was the lipstick Mike felt his mother would enjoy, we purchased it. Then I saw the name—"Reckless Pink"—just what every pastor's wife needs!

I looked around for Steve and located him sampling spray colognes at the other end of the drugstore. Like most parents we had taught Stephen always to point any aerosol spray away from yourself so that you won't get it in your eyes. Stephen was following his teaching perfectly and as a result had filled that end of the drugstore with a foggy mist—an odorous accumulation of about a dozen spray colognes. From the outside, one might have thought a riot was being dispelled with tear gas! I intervened and urged Stephen please to hurry and select one so that we could get out of there while we still had a few friends left. He finally made his choice, but before asking the saleslady to wrap it, I glanced at the name. Again, just what every pastor's wife needs—"Intoxication."

I thought we were finally on our way home when the boys simultaneously spotted a gift in the costume jewelry counter. I have seldom seen such excitement about a little charm bracelet. I suspected they had already seen it and planned to set me up for an additional purchase. Mike went behind the counter, opened it, and pulled out the bracelet. Once again the saleslady nearly experienced a nervous collapse. Excitedly my son showed me the bracelet. It was cheaply made, and I could picture the thing disintegrating within a week or two at the most, so I tried to discourage the purchase, reminding the boys that Martha had a most beautiful charm bracelet and that this additional one would be unnecessary. But loudly they insisted, "She can wear this one to Sunday school."

I couldn't imagine what in the world that had to do with it or why she could wear this bracelet to Sunday school but not any of her other jewelry. Mike and Steve had anticipated my question. "This is a charm bracelet with the Ten Commandments on it!" They stood with pious smugness as I looked at the bracelet. They were correct. Each commandment was engraved on one of the ten separate charms, and the whole thing sold for $1.50. Frankly, it was worth that much just to get out of the store; so we purchased the Ten Commandments charm bracelet.

No three wise men, or unwise men for that matter, ever went bearing three more unusual gifts than we were taking home to Martha for Mother's Day—"Reckless Pink," "Intoxication," and the "Ten Commandments." What a trio!

I managed to get into the house before the boys

so as to forewarn Martha about the celebration she was about to experience. But how can you prepare anyone for the kind of gifts we were bringing? So I stood back as the two boys exploded into the house and began presenting their gifts. All smiles, with huge question marks in her eyes, Martha "ooohed" and "aaahed," spread kisses all around, and said, with near-convincing sincerity, "This is exactly what I wanted. You are both wonderful. I love you."

The boys finally went outside to play, and I tried to regain my shattered equilibrium. Martha and I had fun discussing these unusual gifts and their names. It was really very warm and wonderful. Later that day, we agreed that it was marvelous to see our sons so excited about selecting their own presents for their mother. We allowed our imagination to open some new doors of possibility as we considered the meaning behind the gifts. Every gift reveals much about both the giver and the recipient, for all our gifts have a way of subtly exposing the way we see ourselves and also the way we see the person to whom we are giving our gift. Gifts communicate messages about the nature of the relationship that exists between the giver and the recipient.

The more Martha and I thought about the three gifts that Michael and Stephen had given, and the longer we talked about it, the more we came to see

15

that these boys were "saying" vastly more to their mother than the obvious. Of course, they communicated their love, but they were telling her much more. The gifts uncovered something deep inside them about the way they saw their mother.

I don't believe the boys were conscious of any of the deeper feelings and meanings which motivated them and determined the selection of their gifts, but I am persuaded that Mike and Steve were not just giving Martha lipstick, cologne, and a charm bracelet. They were saying something much more significant and a thousand times more beautiful— they wanted her to look good, to smell good, and to be good! What a colossal combination!

These gifts symbolized in a warmly human way the basic meaning of the supreme gift of God—his Son, Jesus Christ. God gave us his Son to say the obvious, that he loves us and cares for us and that we are constantly in his thoughts. More than anything else God was declaring that he wants us to love him back with all our hearts and minds. But through his gift, God, like Mike and Steve, was also saying something much more profound. He was saying that he wants us to look good, that is, he wants to change the way we appear, the externals of life. God wants to make life more beautiful and more attractive for us.

16

But that's not all. Through God's wonderful gift he was also creating an entirely new atmosphere—a new aroma—in the world. He was showing us that he wants us to receive this new atmosphere for ourselves so that we can become the "carriers," the "spreaders," of this beautiful intoxicating aroma of love throughout the entire earth. Through this great gift of love, poured onto us through Jesus Christ, God is creating a new feeling and a new atmosphere in the world.

But God is not concerned just with external appearance and atmosphere. In a most basic and fundamental way God desires to change the internal structure of our attitudes which form the foundation for our external appearance and atmosphere. God desires more for us than just to "look good" or to "smell good." He wants us to *be* good. He longs to remake our basic nature so that what we do externally is but the natural, free-flowing expression of what we are internally. God is not interested in giving us temporary make-up to cover our faults, nor does he want merely to give repeated applications of some holy cologne designed to disguise the true odor of our lives. God is not a camouflage artist who creates an external veneer of respectability. He moves inside us to the basic source of appearance and atmosphere. There, at the core of our personality, he transforms us so that the way we appear and the atmosphere we create become the natural, normal expressions of our new nature.

Mike and Steve, both created in God's image, felt something deep inside that stimulated them to give gifts which so wonderfully expressed the nature of God within their young lives. And that's good!

Somehow the word *good* has taken on a shallow or weak meaning in the minds of many. This is most unfortunate because the Bible says that "Jesus went about doing good," and I'm certain he would not have wasted his time doing that which was meaningless. Perhaps the word *good* has been downgraded due to a misinterpretation of what the word actually means. Good is not the same as "goody-goody." May the Lord preserve us from that phony, sugary superficiality that some confuse with goodness, for goodness is actually strong and helpful and real.

Some have incorrectly thought of a good man as one who withdraws from life because everything is so evil, a passive spectator whose only contribution is criticism and complaint. Such individuals do nothing and thereby falsely earn the description "good." Goodness is not just the absence of evil, nor is it merely adding up zeros. The true meaning of goodness can be illustrated by a flower garden or a vegetable garden. A garden is not obtained simply by pulling weeds. The weeds must be constantly removed, but something must be planted which, by its very nature, is creative, productive, and alive. Something helpful must grow and bloom if there is to be a garden. It is the same with goodness. Goodness is not attained by withdrawing from the world and refusing to do this or that. Goodness means that a new quality or ingredient, something creative, positive, and alive, has been planted in our lives and is constantly growing, producing flowers to beautify and fruit to strengthen.

When the Lord endeavors to make us look good, smell good, and be good, he does not try to subtract us from life or remove us from the real world. God wants us to live and be involved in the world so that in us and then through us he can place in the world an ingredient, an attitude, a force, and a power that, without his life in us, would be totally absent. This means a great deal more than just an improved outward appearance. If we are to look good in the way God judges beauty, then everything we are externally must be an accurate demonstration of the new, living beauty of Christ that has been created in us. Our outward appearance becomes the means whereby the internal goodness and beauty of Christ is communicated to the world.

External religiosity cannot camouflage internal

iniquity. Someone said, "The gods men worship write their names on their faces." Once a man comes to know the goodness of God through Jesus Christ and tastes the grace and love of God, everything about his appearance begins progressively to improve. The internal transformation begins to show. God writes his name on the person's face, and the person begins to look good. And that *is* good.

But Mike and Steve also gave Martha a beautiful cologne called "Intoxication." Anyone who knows Martha realizes that the boys did not give her this gift because she was oblivious to some "problem—" she is extremely beautiful and refined in every way. Mike and Steve were saying that they wanted Martha to continue to exude an atmosphere of beauty and vitality and excitement. And she does! Steve's selection was a little boy's attempt to tell his mother that he loved her and that he wanted her to be really alive. And she is!

The cologne carried a fascinating name—"Intoxication." How the world needs a tonic of love and life! "Mother," the boys were saying, "we want you to continue to be a tonic, to permeate our home with an atmosphere, a feeling, a spirit of invigorating excitement."

We are not often conscious of it, but atmosphere is very influential. Some people are exciting to be around, even for a few short moments. Even in brief conversation they exude an electrifying atmosphere. They seem to have an extra "touch" of life about them.

Then there are those pitiable people who unfortunately feel called to carry around in their personalities those dark clouds of doom and gloom; they drip with complaints and criticisms. These sad people fill the atmosphere around them with a sticky, drizzling fog of negativism and depression.

All of us create one atmosphere or the other. Within our attitudes we produce the "spiritual weather" that moves across the terrain of our personal worlds.

Two women were talking over the back fence, and one of them commented on the weather. "My, isn't this a beautiful day?" The other replied, "Yes, but it's raining somewhere." For some people, it is always raining somewhere. Constantly complaining, they murder every happy moment with a cold, withering blast of disapproval.

But Jesus Christ is not like this! He does not produce negativism and depression in peoples' lives! He comes as a divine tonic! He turns us on! He gives us excitement and vitality! He invigorates and inspires! He intoxicates us with the wine of his Spirit.

21

On the Day of Pentecost when thousands accepted Christ as Savior, the people who had gathered to hear and see the disciples of Christ accused them of being drunk! Simon Peter quickly retorted that they were not drunk since it was only nine o'clock in the morning. Obviously Simon, the Big Fisherman, knew the habits of a drinking man. "But," he said in explanation, "we are men who have been filled with the new wine of the Spirit of the living Christ who conquered death and the grave. We are God-intoxicated men." What had created the impression that they were drunk? The Spirit of Christ within the disciples had so penetrated the atmosphere that the people felt themselves attracted to Christ by the vitality and enthusiasm which he had created within his friends and followers. These followers were so excited and elated about what Christ had done in their lives that they gave the impression to the casual observer that they were drunk.

General Booth, the founder of the Salvation Army, once said something to the effect that the more he was with some Christians the better he liked sinners. I know exactly what he was talking about. It is extremely difficult for me to accept the fact that people who have met Jesus Christ and have come to experience the fantastic grace of God and the forgiveness of their sins can be sour-souled prophets and grim-faced lecturers. I believe the exact opposite is true! Genuine Christians who know they are redeemed sinners are alive with the intoxicating Spirit of God. These men and women permeate the atmosphere of their homes and offices and schools with the intoxicating aroma of faith, hope, and love.

Mike and Steve joined to give Martha a third gift —the little charm bracelet inscribed with the Ten Commandments. With this present they were non-verbally and unconsciously affirming that in addition to their desire for Martha to look good and to smell good, down deep inside her life they wanted her to be good. Below the level of conscious thought, Mike and Steve were affirming that they wanted Martha to be certain that the inside of the cup of life was clean so that these two other appealing attributes of appearance and atmosphere would not be a cover-up for an unhealthy and unholy nature. From their heart of hearts, where deepest hopes and longings dwell and are expressed through spontaneous gestures, they were symbolically declaring that they wanted these two outward expressions of beauty and aroma to be the natural, normal expressions of an internal beauty and spirit that was created and placed inside her life by the living Christ. In other words, "Mother, we want you to be good. We want goodness to be your basic nature, your true spirit, your actual attitude."

Truth does not exist until it comes to life in every-day encounters. Truth does not exist in the abstract. We have all heard Burt Bacharach's song, "What the world needs now is love, sweet love." Others say that what the world needs is truth, while another declares that what the world needs is honesty. The world does need love, truth, and honesty, but these values do not float around as disembodied spirits. If there is going to be more love in the world, then I must be more loving. If there is to be more truth and honesty, then I must be more truthful and more honest. It is impossible for these values to exist apart from their incarnation in my life and relationships.

Michael and Stephen unknowingly expressed an exciting truth that many people have not consciously realized. Great and lasting values must be embodied in us and personalized through us or these values do not and will not exist.

God created a world in which eternal truth must be personalized to be recognized. He realized that if his eternal love was ever to be conveyed to others he must put this truth in a body, in a person. This love which God has for his creation and for every individual must be incarnated in flesh or it is not recognizable and realizable. So God did just that in

24

his Son, Jesus Christ. God's gift to the world is a loving and eternal God personalizing himself in a human body so that all of us can know him who is "the way, the truth, and the life."

Since the man Jesus Christ came into the world as a visible expression of the living God, we must look at Jesus Christ to know what God is like. Jesus is not like God; God is like Jesus. The full and final revelation of the nature of God is communicated to the world in the individual person of Jesus Christ. If we accept by faith this gift of God in Jesus Christ, he will give to every one of us a new appearance, a new atmosphere, and a new nature.

In the following pages we're going to look first at the man Christ Jesus, the full revelation of God. He is the only means whereby we can know what God is like, and Jesus reveals what we can do to meet and know God personally. We are going to see the kind of person Jesus was and how he, through everyday contacts and relationships, totally embodied the nature of God and how he communicates this embodied truth to us. We are going to look at the man Jesus Christ who came riding triumphantly into Jerusalem and into the world . . . on a donkey.

We will meet three people who beautifully represent what happens when a person meets Jesus Christ. We will see God's truth of transforming power personalized in their lives. We will walk and live with them and watch while Jesus Christ transfigures one's appearance, alters the atmosphere of another, and is the means whereby the actions of still another are entirely changed and redirected.

In all of this I believe we will begin to discover some exciting, living representations of the Christian experience. I hope we will recognize some new and urgently needed symbols of the Christian life embodied in these three transformed individuals. As a result of our reacquaintance with these people, we may realize that we can appropriate the same living attributes and qualities into our daily lives. By accepting the man Jesus Christ, the supreme gift of God, every one of us can look good, smell good, and be good! Without exception, all of us can have an improved appearance, an enthusiastic and invigorating spirit, and a changed nature which will inspire new actions and activities. This can happen to us!

So come along to meet the Man who can enter your life and mine and give us his version of "Reckless Pink," "Intoxication," and the "Ten Commandments." Michael and Stephen were saying to Martha what God has been saying all along—he wants us to look good, smell good, and be good. And that *is* good.

The Man
on the
Donkey

JUST AS A touch of truth came to life and walked around in Mike and Steve and Martha in everyday events, so eternal truth came fully and beautifully to life and walked around in the everyday experiences of a man working in a carpenter's shop, a happy crowd celebrating a wedding, a fisherman and a tax collector.

The people about whom you will read in these pages were real. There is nothing fictitious about them. They were genuine, red-blooded, living, laughing, loving people with the same mixture of hope and fear, dreams and frustrations, as you and I. Neither they nor their experiences were created by someone's imagination. And the most encouraging fact of all is that what they were, we are, and what they became, we can become.

As you meet them, you will feel an instantaneous identification. Something deep inside you will reach out to them, and you will know and understand them. They will become your lifelong friends.

The main person in this story was a real man with all the compassion and considerateness necessary to a genuine friendship. You could relax with him and talk about the most intimate, personal matters in your life. Even though he might not approve of all you did, he would never make you feel hopeless about yourself or cause you to feel rejected. You would like to fish or play golf with this man; you would like to sit over a cup of coffee with him and talk, long into the night. After the conversation, you would discover something new and different about your life. Deep inside you would feel yourself beginning to change.

It is said that distance lends enchantment. Generally this is true, but distance can sometimes lend detachment. The tendency to romanticize the past often contributes to a subtle depersonalization of those exciting individuals who actually lived years ago and walked and worked in the real world with tired feet and sweaty bodies.

This inclination to unreality has been especially true in regard to the people whose lives are recorded in the Bible. Often they are presented as bloodless, burdenless, fleshless statues—not anything like us mortals made of common clay. We resist even the idea that they were cut from the same cloth as we. Rather, we see them as tailor-made and everyone else as the mail-order variety.

This practice of depersonalizing the people of the Bible has distorted our picture of the real human beings we are going to meet in this book. This is especially true of the man who is the friend of all us clay-footed travelers, our main subject—Jesus.

For some strange reason we put on rose-colored glasses to look at him. Why we persist in this perplexes me. Is the thought that Jesus was a *real* man somehow too much for us to accept? The fact that all his emotions and feelings were as strong and real as ours may simply be too staggering a thought for us to take. To defend against this we retreat into a make-believe world populated with plastic people —a kind of biblical Disneyland.

The Bible says that Jesus was "in all points tempted like as we are" (Heb. 4:15, KJV), but we don't really believe that. This idea is so threatening that we are tempted to push it out of our minds by

31

making Jesus into a Superman who floats around and above the nitty-gritty world in cool detachment. We picture him as the unmoved mover who sits above it all, alone with the stars.

To be sure, he was the Son of God, but he somehow laid aside that divinity and, as Paul said, "took upon him the form of a servant." The word translated "form" literally means "essential nature." Paul says Jesus took on the essential nature of a servant. In other words, he was not playing a part in someone's drama; he was thoroughly and totally man, subject to all the temptations and vicissitudes that stalk every other member of the human race. Therefore in spite of our resistance, it is nevertheless true that Jesus was real.

Yes, Jesus was real. His hunger was real; his hair was real. The blood he bled when he worked at the carpenter's bench in Nazareth and the blood he bled when he died on the cross in Jerusalem was real. His loneliness, muscles, tears, teeth—everything— were real.

Far too many have extracted the flesh and blood from their Bibles with the deleterious result that people in the Scripture seem so anemic—antiseptic and unreal. Consequently we have difficulty accepting the Bible as the fact—the reality—that it was and is. In our sanitized minds we imagine that Jesus' clothes were always spotless, his fingernails clean, his hair neatly cut and combed, and his body subtly suggesting a touch of "English Leather."

Why do we do this? To avoid the confrontation with reality that would shatter our fairyland fantasies. To escape the world, we take to the plastic wings of imagination. To prevent any unsettling effect upon our delicate feelings, we engage in every evasive tactic conceivable. To avoid the agony of realism, even in our religion (especially in our religion), we cover Jesus with sugary unreality and push him back into history, up into heaven, or ahead into some future kingdom—anywhere but on a real cross made of real wood with a real human body stapled to it. This is too much for our refined taste, and so we cry, "Do something with that gory cross; cover it with gold or silver or lilies or anything . . . just change it . . . perfume it, wash it off, do something, but change it." And many churches have complied.

It is true that Jesus was crucified "from the foundation of the world" (Rev. 13:8, KJV), that Calvary was in God's heart from the beginning. However, our preoccupation with the Christ of history and our emphasis upon his crucifixion "from the foundation of the world" has tended to diminish the fact that Jesus Christ was crucified *somewhere*. It really happened outside Jerusalem on a hill—blood, cursing, crosses, flies, spears, filth, stench, and all—not in some antiseptic cloister but on a contaminated cross sandwiched between two thieves and overlooking a crap game.

Our difficulty in comprehending this reality is compounded by the fact that so many of us spend most of our time sitting in air-conditioned comfort, sipping "tall cool ones," and talking in vague abstractions about unimportant matters. Consequently we can't hear this man, or any man for that matter, when he cries, "I thirst." Rather than even try to hear, we make every effort not to, with the result that our capacity to hear dies, our emotions dry up, and Jesus becomes a plastic statue or a transparent figure on a church wall whose only stain is in the cold glass that falsely depicts him.

Join with me in making an honest attempt to let the stark reality of Christ and the factual events leading up to his death really tear into our insides with a new wave of engulfing love. Let the warm waters of feeling sweep over the dry sands of propriety.

Remember, if God hadn't cared, there never would have been a cross in the first place. If God had not felt and wept and agonized, there never would have been a Calvary. If God could feel that deeply about us, can we feel any less deeply about him and about the world he loved and for which he died?

It is difficult to understand Jesus—who he was and what he wanted to do. Even his first followers had trouble comprehending him, and I don't blame them. I am still trying to understand it with my mind and feel it with my spirit, and I have the advantage of about two thousand years of Christian history along with written records to help me.

The Bible says, in Luke 22:24, that the disciples began to argue among themselves as to who would have the highest rank in the coming kingdom. Who was going to be the vice-president in charge of missions, the vice-president in charge of miracles, the vice-president in charge of money? We may smile at their misguided ambitions, but the church has been discussing the same irrelevant questions for years. We smile because we see ourselves and also because we wouldn't want anyone to see us weep, which is what we should be doing because of our misdirected desires and our distorted priorities.

In this self-seeking atmosphere Jesus told his disciples that "in this world the kings and great men order their slaves around, and the slaves have no choice but to like it! But among you, the one who serves you best will be your leader. Out in the world the master sits at the table and is served by his servants. But not here!" said Jesus (Luke 22:25–27, LB). The kings of the world, beginning with the first and coming to the present moment—potentates, princes, presidents, premiers—are all consumed with one desire—power. They employ words dripping with political sugar to conceal the ugly ' reality of their insatiable lust. The pitch is that if they are in control it will be good for the rest of us. But don't be fooled. History teaches, but humanity doesn't learn that the kings of the world have all lusted after dominion and control.

The kingdoms of the world are built upon the foundation of a consuming lust for power, and the landlord of the kingdoms of this world is Beelzebub. This is why he could offer the kingdoms of the world to Christ in that agonizing confrontation in the wilderness. Satan couldn't tempt Jesus with something he didn't have, and he has the kingdoms of the world. Therefore don't be surprised when you find that they are built upon greed, lust, lying, and hatred. That's the way the kingdoms of the world have always been and always will be until the kingdoms of this world become the kingdom of our Lord and Savior Jesus Christ. The kingdoms of *this* world reflect the attitudes and ambitions of their landlord, Beelzebub.

But in Mark 11 we read of a new kind of king, establishing a new kind of kingdom.

As they neared Bethphage and Bethany on the outskirts of Jerusalem and came to the Mount of Olives, Jesus sent two of his disciples on ahead.

"Go into that village over there," he told them, "and just as you enter you will see a colt tied up that has never been ridden. Untie him and bring him here. And if anyone asks you what you are doing, just say, 'Our Master needs him and will return him soon.' "

Off went the two men and found the colt standing in the street, tied outside a house. As they were untying it, some who were standing there demanded, "What are you doing, untying the colt?"

So they said what Jesus had told them to, and then the men agreed.

So the colt was brought to Jesus and the disciples threw their cloaks across its back for him to ride on. Then many in the crowd spread out their coats along the road before him, while others threw down leafy branches from the fields (Mark 11:1–8, LB).

Look at him! There he was "in the center of the procession with the crowds ahead . . . behind"—everywhere—"and all shouting, 'Hail to the King!' 'Praise God for him who comes in the name of the Lord!' . . . 'Praise God for the return of our father David's kingdom . . .' 'Hail to the King of the universe!' " (Mark 11:9–10, LB).

Here comes the King of kings, riding on a donkey! Such a drastic departure from the usual practice must surely be significant. In biblical history the only time any king ever rode on a donkey was when he was coming in peace. But since the kings of the world are only interested in power, we can understand how seldom they ever came in peace. They usually ride on white horses, or in glistening chariots, or in big Cadillacs. Caesars don't ride bicycles, and never donkeys.

Most of the kingdoms of this world are built upon flagrant, horrendous sins like Hitler's Reich that was supposed to last a thousand years. Like the false kingdoms before and after, it was built upon hatred, prejudice, murder, imagined superiority, and the lust for power. It ended as all the kingdoms of this world will end, ignominiously, with a suicide in a Berlin bunker. The white horse threw his rider; the chariot turned over; the Cadillac exploded.

Many of the world's Caesars may be more subtle

than Hitler, but the ultimate outcome is always the same. Sin inevitably creates a delusion that confuses power with strength and applause with approval, and the kings belatedly discover that their shaky crown slowly "becomes a crown of lead that makes to swoon the aching head that wears it."

The kingdoms of this world will come to the same end, for they are built upon the foundation of sinking sand. "The rise and fall of twenty-one great civilizations exegetes the text, 'The wages of sin is death,'" Arnold Toynbee reminds us. How good the optimistic hopes for a better world sound—the New Deal, the Fair Deal, the New Frontier, the Great Society. They're humanistic and idealistic, they just never work. Yet people keep falling for their promises even though they recognize the same old faded hopes dressed up in new slogans.

For how many generations have we heard our leaders say that we are "on the verge of an era of peace"? What a cruel hoax. There is no peace—not now, not tomorrow, not ever—as long as the kings of this world are in charge.

With much pomp and pageantry the world's leaders meet again at the summit to make glittering promises of peace on earth. What a sad show! They are only rearranging the deck chairs on the Titanic.

The Society of International Law released some

interesting statistics: "Out of 3800 years of recorded history there have been only 268 years of actual peace, and during that period of time, there have been over 8000 peace treaties signed." There certainly has been a lot of tobacco wasted in peace pipes, hasn't there?

The kingdoms of this world will pass into the graveyard of civilizations, and if we put our faith in these kings and their kingdoms, it will be tragically misplaced. If we put our ultimate confidence in the leaders of this world, it will be a frustrating exercise in disillusionment. Build castles on the beach of human dreams, and, like children by the sea, watch them melt away under the relentless tides of man's tempestuous transgressions.

Napoleon said, "Caesar, Alexander, Charlemagne, and I have founded empires. Upon what did we rest the creation of our genius? Upon force. Jesus Christ, alone, founded his empire upon love, and today millions would die for him. I die before my time and my body will be given to the worms. Such is the fate of him who has been called the great Napoleon. What an eternal abyss between my deep misery and the eternal kingdom of Christ which is loved, proclaimed, adored throughout the whole world. Call you this dying? No. He is rather living."

You are right, Napoleon! He *is* living, and he lives

as the only king worthy of our ultimate and undivided devotion.

If Napoleon finally saw this irrevocable truth, why can't we? Why can't the leaders of this world? Because lust for power, like any lust, produces a blindness to reality. With our short-sighted craving for temporary materialistic satisfaction, we let "the blind lead the blind." May God open our eyes before we all "fall into a ditch!" Pray for the healing of our blindness so that all may see the only king worthy of our total dedication—Jesus Christ. May all of us see that he is real and living and that he comes riding on that donkey and into our lives to produce the only era of peace we will ever know in this life and in this world.

The carpenter rides relentlessly through the wreckage of Jerusalem, the collapse of Rome, and the rise and fall of civilization after civilization. Coming in peace, he presents a devastating picture, a judgment on man's pretenses to power.

Have you ever wondered why he rode a donkey that had never before been ridden? It was not coincidental. In 1 Samuel 6:7, God tells the people to prepare a carriage for the Ark of the Covenant, a box containing the Ten Commandments and Aaron's rod. The ark was the symbol of God's presence with his people, and this awe-inspiring object was to be borne on a carriage that had never been used before for any purpose. The animals that were to draw this new carriage were never to have been used before.

Jesus told his followers to secure a donkey that had never before been ridden. Why? Because he, the Ark of the New Covenant, was about to ride into Jerusalem. Jesus Christ—the Ark of the New Testament, the living presence of God with his people, the New Covenant, the fulfillment of the promises of God—was to be carried into Jerusalem on an animal that had never been used before!

In Exodus 25 we read God's instructions on the construction of the Ark of the Covenant. It was to have a lid of pure gold 3¾ feet long and 2¼ feet wide. This lid was the place of forgiveness for the sins of the people—the mercy seat of God. Here sin would be forgiven and lives cleansed. God says, "I will meet you there and talk with you from above the place of mercy between the cherubim; and the Ark will contain the laws of my covenant. There I will tell you my commandments for the people of Israel" (Exodus 25:22, LB). Here is where God met and talked with his people. It was the place of law, mercy, and continuing communication.

Jesus' ride into Jerusalem on Palm Sunday takes on dramatically explosive consequences for all mankind. The words of Exodus and Samuel, the law and the prophets, are literally fulfilled. All the loving purposes of God for man's redemption are fulfilled.

In Christ, the Ark of the New Covenant, there is peace and mercy. He is the living and continuing Word of God. These blessings are in Christ and in him alone.

Our Jewish friends stand at the Wailing Wall in Jerusalem, the western wall of the old Temple and all that remains of that ancient edifice. They stand there to weep and to pray. Beyond the wall lies the old Temple area where the Jewish faithful refuse to walk for fear that they might step over the spot where the Ark of the Covenant lies buried in the rubble and debris of history's desolations. They believe that if they walk over the ark they will die.

We Christians feel a sincere respect for their devotion but deep compassion for their misdirection because we know that the ark of the real covenant does not lie buried anywhere. Jesus Christ, God's Ark of the New Covenant, was raised from death and, as the living Savior, comes to us at our own personal "wailing wall" to say, "Be not afraid, it is I."

The veil in the Temple which enclosed the place the Ark of the Covenant would occupy, if it could have been found, was torn from the top to the bottom when Christ died on the cross. God himself destroyed the veil that separated the Holy of Holies, the place for the Ark of the Covenant, from the outside world, for when Jesus Christ, the Ark of the New Covenant, died, the old ark was obsolete and unnecessary. Christ fulfilled the law and the prophets and became the mercy seat and means of forgiveness. In Christ, God and man meet and talk. The Ark of the New Covenant, Jesus Christ, is alive forever. In triumph he rides into every man's life, bringing peace with God, self, and others.

The Man on that donkey is riding still, through the complicated liturgies of today's religions that have buried God in ritualism. He rides through the jungles of materialism which slick-tongued advertisers call progress and through all the systems and cultures that degrade and destroy the "little ones." The Man on that donkey still rides down the streets of the world, and the volcaniclike reverberations that follow the quiet steps of the donkey will eventually bring down all the kingdoms of this world.

The man Jesus Christ came into the lives of some people in his day and brought them his magnificent peace. He led them away from the wailing walls of frustration to a life of festive wedding parties. By demonstrating what happens when God is allowed to enter a life, he completely changed the idea of what it meant to be religious. The appearance, atmosphere, and actions of some of the people who admitted him into their lives have become parables of what it means to be a Christian, to live a happy and holy life, to be genuinely religious. They are symbols of what it means to look good, smell good, and be good.

Some everyday people just like ourselves met the Man on that donkey, and their lives were dramatically changed. They have become examples of what happens to a person when he becomes a follower of the Man, and the expressions of love which they gave Christ have created some beautiful symbols which show us more of what it means to be a follower of the Man.

These symbols are not new; they have only been ignored and overlooked by Christians who found it more comfortable to use cold, dead symbols rather than living, continuing ones. The outline of a fish, a metal cross, or some Greek letters arranged on the wall all "say" something to be sure, but the communication is so sterile, so lifeless. The symbols we will rediscover are not cold and impersonal. They are vital, vibrant, and exciting. They are reckless and intoxicating. They live.

The real people we will be meeting and the symbols they created can be an exciting part of our daily lives. They are not "things" imprisoned in cold marble or dead metal. They are not just something you wear; they are something you are. These are not objects you can put on, but attitudes you can't take off.

What happened to these people can happen to us. They are our representatives, and through the eyes of their experience, we perceive how marvelous life can be.

Throw
Away
the
Garbage

IT SOUNDS incredible and astounding, but it is nonetheless true—Jesus, the Man on the donkey, came to set men free! He came to liberate us from the Caesars of the world, but even more important and necessary, he came to liberate us from the totalitarianism of death and the grave.

The Man on the donkey once said he came to bring release and relief for the captives. To be sure, he meant political captives, but more than that, he meant relief for all who are enslaved by the shackles of unbelief and the manacles of meaninglessness. He came to give life and to give it abundantly! He came to make all of life "look good."

He declared that "I, when I am lifted up from the earth, will draw all men to myself" (John 12:32,

49

RSV). I am persuaded that the only reason we are interested in Jesus at all and the only reason we even consider Christianity is because Jesus took the initiative by intentionally moving into the path of our existence. He invaded our lives in such a loving way that we now feel powerfully attracted to him. Both the intellectual and emotional impressions which we feel urging us to commit our lives completely to him are caused by the Spirit of God. Therefore we should not be reluctant to respond in the beginning simply because we do not understand everything about the process and its conclusion. We must remember that what we feel knocking on the door of our mind is the Spirit of Jesus Christ, the best friend we will ever have, who is anxious to enter our lives. This Man is presently drawing us into his circle of friends, and surely we will not delay responding to such a promising invitation.

The Man on the donkey comes to us in real, lasting peace. He is not coming to fight with us or to put us down; he is not going to take the spark out of living, for he is certainly not the world's great kill-joy. He has not come to destroy life but to give life and to give it abundantly (John 10:10).

If only we would allow the Man on the donkey to set us free, he would liberate us, forgive our sin, remove our guilt, and unravel our tensions. He would do this, for he has promised to, and he is a man of his word. He will keep his promise. If only we would turn loose and throw the garment of our faith down before him, waving branches of devotion as we exaltedly open the gates of our lives, he would enter in peace just as he entered Jerusalem two thousand years ago. He would enter our hearts, bringing life and joy forever.

In John 11 we have the record of Lazarus, one of the people whose life was entered and changed by the Man. Lazarus, the friend of Jesus and the brother of Mary and Martha, had died. The family had lived together in Bethany and were all friends of Jesus. Since Jesus was not present when Lazarus died, Mary and Martha sent him word of their sorrow. After a brief delay, Jesus returned to Bethany, but by the time he arrived, Lazarus had been dead four days and was already buried.

We are all just as dead as Lazarus. We may be physically alive, mentally alert, and emotionally sensitive, but we are spiritually dead. Every area of life is touched by the pale, clammy hand of death. Everything in us and about us is influenced by death's thorough permeation. Every thought is touched; every relationship affected. Since we are all spiritually dead, Lazarus becomes a picture of every man.

But Lazarus is not the only dead person in this story. Others around him were also "dead." Although their death was not evidenced in the same way as Lazarus's, they were nonetheless dead—confined and limited to some form of grave and grave clothes. Jesus came back to Bethany, not only to call Lazarus out of the grave, but also to call Martha and Mary, their friends, the scribes and the Pharisees, everyone, to a new life.

That day Bethany was a microcosm of the entire world. Looking at those people, we see ourselves more clearly. Some people are dead emotionally. Somewhere along the way they were made ashamed of their feelings, possibly when someone implied that emotion was undignified or unintellectual. Becoming self-conscious and afraid of their feelings, they buried them somewhere deep inside. They now lead straight, proper, controlled lives marked by decorum and propriety, but they are dusty tombs with little or no light, vitality, or love.

Others are mentally dead. Great thoughts and new ideas no longer stretch the muscles of their minds. The windows are never opened to allow the cool breezes of fresh truth to blow through the musty rooms of prejudice. The mind stays closed, locked, and dark.

Some are mentally dead; some, emotionally dead;

but all are spiritually dead. In Bethany Jesus called everybody to life, and in the same way he now calls each of us from the limiting, confining, depressing forms of death that imprison us.

What are some of the attributes and expressions of death from which Christ would save us? What are the characteristics of the grave? Some are painfully obvious. The inability to respond, to grow, and to develop is death. The eyes no longer sparkle in response to others; the mind no longer quickens with the stimulus of new ideas; the body serves as the pallbearer for two dear but dead friends—heart and soul.

And then the grave? Have you ever looked into an open grave? What a chilling thing it is—a dark, little, narrow space that pinches and confines and imprisons. How smothering and suffocating it would be to be buried partially alive. The thought is terrifying, but millions *are* buried alive, and the awfulness is intensified when we realize how many bury themselves. They dig their own graves and pull the earth in over them.

When we look at the world around us or when we take a quick look inside ourselves, we can see manifestations of death and the grave everywhere. Having become so accustomed to their presence, we have almost lost the capacity to see them for what they really are. Death and the grave have so permeated life in all its forms that many have lost the capacity for recognition, let alone resistance. Occasionally something inside us may rise up to resist the dominance of death and the gravelike mentality that fills our world, but then we fall weakly back into the old and easy ruts that in time deepen into a grave themselves, for depth is the only difference between a rut and a grave. The death that surrounds us slowly begins to reach out with its clammy fingers to touch and destroy all of life.

That day in Bethany there was no question about the death of Lazarus. He was dead and everyone knew it. However, some others in Bethany were also dead but didn't know it. The attributes of death and the grave were unconsciously dominating the lives of the family and friends of Lazarus. They needed new life as much as Lazarus. His death was obvious and theirs was not—a most subtle and dangerous difference.

When Jesus returned to Bethany, Martha went out to meet him. Through the beautiful conversation between them, the Lord worked to bring Martha into a personal faith that is alive to God in the present. Martha's faith was confident of the past and the future, but she was nearly dead to the life

54

of faith in the present. Her faith was in yesterday and tomorrow—very little in today. But enough of that small spark of faith in the present was lying unnoticed and undernourished in her heart so that with the stimulus of Jesus Christ it could be ignited into a bright flame.

Martha said, "If you had been here, my brother would not have died" (John 11:21, RSV). That is a true statement, but it represents faith in the power of God only in the past. It is living in yesterday. All of us need the kind of faith that has been developed through the experiences of the past, both our experiences and the experiences of those people recorded in the Bible. A faith rooted in the realities of history is helpful and necessary, but we cannot live on another's faith any more than we can live on pictures of food. We need both food and faith in the present moment! We can learn from the past and should, but we cannot live in the past. Lot's wife tried it and died, and so will we if we live exclusively in the past. You can't drive a car successfully if you spend *all* your time looking intently into the rear-view mirror.

But Martha began to emerge from the darkness of despair caused by a "yesterday" faith, and a small spark of hope and faith in the present began to fill her thoughts. She replied, "But even now I know that whatever you ask from God, God will give you" (John 11:22, RSV).

The light was breaking! Jesus recognized this spark of hope and faith, and he poured onto it the flammable fuel of his promise for the present. Jesus' words seemed to explode with excitement when Martha discovered the presence of this mustard seed of faith that lay dormant in the soil of her soul. Christ exclaimed, "Your brother will rise again!" Martha was staggered by his word. It was almost too much to comprehend or accept, and she tried to avoid its implications by escaping into the future. How natural, and how much like us!

Martha replied, "I know that he will rise again in the resurrection at the last day" (John 11:24, RSV). So there it is; that was her faith. It was in the past and in the future. She was alive to yesterday and tomorrow; she had faith in the God of history and in the God of heaven but very little in the God of the present.

Jesus encouraged Martha to see that she could have a vital, living, transforming, death-conquering faith today. He helped her and us and all the world by making the greatest statement ever uttered: "I am the resurrection and the life . . . and whoever lives and believes in me shall never die" (John 11:25–26,

RSV). Like the sound of a trumpet, God's words of deliverance attack the dungeons of hell to throw open the cell doors of hopelessness, liberating men from darkness and fear and sin and death. The fantastic truth is that he was talking to all of us, not just to Martha or Lazarus, but to you and to me.

Jesus declared that we do not have to live in the dusty past or in the distant future; we can live now in the triumphant presence of the eternal "I am." We don't have to choose between the "I was" or the "I will be," but we are called by the "I am."

Jesus further declared that he will provide us with continuous resources right now if we will only take him at his word. Many of us are unnecessarily paralyzed by the erroneous idea that God works only in the past, that he is limited, if not totally absent, from the present. Many "believe" that God did great things for Moses, Elijah, David, Simon Peter, Paul, and all the rest, but they were different. It was easier in their day when life was simpler and men were more religiously inclined. Some feel that the complex, computerized society of today is too complicated for us *and* for God.

At the other extreme are those who "believe" that God will do great things in the future when he comes again. To them God's only power is in the future tense. The dramatic demonstration of God's power witnessed in the past and the power God will reveal in the future are unavailable today. Our technological graves are too deep, our cultural tombs too dark for God to do anything but wring his hands in frustration, vainly hoping man will change and come back, as though God is always "back" somewhere in yesterday or "out" somewhere in tomorrow. Many in the church, and even more in the world, lie back, corpselike, in the grave of unexpectation to wait, totally unbelieving that God could be "in" their todays.

Many find themselves existing in a paralyzed parenthesis with an absentee God. He expended most of his power in "the good ol' days" and is now retired from active participation, hoping to regain his depleted energy so as to return in the fading seconds of the game of life to win the contest for his defeated followers.

But suddenly the Man on that donkey appears, proclaiming, "I am the resurrection. I am the life. I am the power and victory. I am now!" The "I am" who is the same "yesterday, today, and forever" is on the scene today.

In Bethany Jesus called Lazarus from the grave of total death, but he also called Martha from the partial death of unresponsiveness and from a preoccupation with yesterday and tomorrow. What

Jesus did for Martha, he had, in an even greater way, to do for Mary.

Mary was immobilized in grief. In his typically understanding way, Jesus sent for her. "Go tell Mary I want to see her." In response to the word of Jesus, Mary walked out of her tomb of despair much as Lazarus was to walk out of his tomb momentarily. Mary went at once to Jesus, another example of the magnetic power of Christ to call people out from graves of grief, doubt, fear, and hopelessness. *All* graves open to his command.

Mary came to Jesus and despairingly cried, "If you had been here, my brother would still be alive" (John 11:32, LB). She was overwhelmed by sorrow and shackled by the graveclothes of grief and, thinking only of the past, cried words that have been the sad lament of millions—"If only." Typical of so many, Mary was engulfed by regrets, fruitlessly repeating, "If only, if only." How tragic to see so many "Marys" confined to that dusty, dreary grave of despair which a preoccupation with the past always digs.

The friends of Mary and Martha had also buried their faith in the same cemetery of hopelessness. The pall of deathlike attitudes that had descended on Bethany elicited from Jesus one of the few instances of indignation we find reported from his life. What was it that caused him to be "moved with indignation and deeply troubled" (John 11:33, LB)? I feel it was the same problem which caused Jesus to be disturbed by his faithless followers when he cried, "Oh, faithless generation, how long am I to be with you?" (Mark 9:19, RSV). After so many fulfilled promises, so many confirming miracles, so many years of demonstrated power, Christ was understandably disturbed with his followers' addiction to death and defeat. There he was—the Son of God with power over life, death, disease, depression, guilt, everything—and his followers still burdened themselves with destructive masochism. They refused to let their minds be lifted out of the ruts of unbelief; they refused to relinquish their love of suffering.

Since most of us resemble the people in Bethany, I imagine that Christ is as displeased with us as he was with them. If anything, *our* guilt is greater because we have the example of their experience as our guide. It is tragic that after all Christ has done for us we still find ourselves so inordinately preoccupied with defeat, despair, and death.

Christ came to Bethany to call Mary from her grave of hopelessness as surely as he came to call Lazarus from his. Both needed life and deliverance from the confinement of a tomb. Mary was imprisoned in her house of sorrow, gazing through dark windows onto the misty moors of yesterday. Desperately she needed to be called out to view the sunlit mountains of faith and life. Lazarus needed to be called from his grave just as did Martha, Mary, and their friends; *all* needed to be released from their own personal prisons, for all were dead. The difference was only in degree.

As Jesus, standing tall and erect, faced the tomb of Lazarus, a large crowd gathered. Many were there including Martha, Mary, their mourning friends, and people who had been attracted along the way as this strange procession made a return trip to the cemetery. Most processions go to the cemetery to bury a dead body, but this one went to bring back a living one. He was to be exhumed by the living God! Only one person in the crowd actually knew what was going to happen, but isn't it comforting that he does know what is going to occur?

When the crowd arrived at the tomb of Lazarus, Jesus unexpectedly commanded the people to roll away the stone that covered the entrance. Why didn't Jesus roll away the stone with his own mighty words? If he could call a dead man back to life with his "word," why couldn't he remove a stone? The reason is, I believe, that Christ never does anything by a miracle that can be done without it. Removing the stone was something the people could do, and

Christ always utilizes human instrumentality to accomplish his work. When we do what man can do, then God does what man cannot do. Since removing the stone was something the people could do, Christ commanded them to do it. Returning Lazarus to life was something only Christ could do, and so, through the opening created by man's obedience, he called Lazarus back to life.

We cannot coerce men to follow Christ or force them to accept the life he gives, but we can remove the obstacles that inhibit the flow of his word, and we can be the instruments through which his life-giving Spirit works. When we do all that Christ commands, then he will do that which we cannot do: give life to dead men!

Lazarus was not just mentally or emotionally dead; he was totally dead. There was nothing he could do for himself. In this sense Lazarus is the picture of every man, for without Christ we are all spiritually, totally dead.

God says that we are sinners and that "the wages of sin is death" (Rom. 6:23, KJV). He also says that we are dead in sin (Eph. 1:2)—not just *in* sin, but *dead* in sin. We are like a boat that is not just in the water but "dead" in the water. We are not like a boat whose motor is working or whose sails are up; we are "dead" in the water of life, and the waves of waywardness and the storms of sensuality lash against us as we "go under" and the frail craft of our flesh slowly sinks into a watery grave.

But someone says, "Wait a minute! I'm not totally dead because I have some good feelings and do some very good things." No doubt this is true. Nevertheless, the Bible still says that we are dead in sin, totally depraved, and there is no good thing in us (Rom. 7:18). The Scripture teaches and human nature undeniably confirms this fact.

To be totally depraved does not mean that we are so evil as to be incapable of some exceptionally good and helpful deeds. This is not what the Bible teaches, but it does say that every aspect of life has been influenced by evil. It declares that not a single area of life remains untouched and untainted by sin. Man's life is not totally evil, but the totality of life has been touched by evil.

Even that part of our lives which we think of as "good" has been permeated by the virus of selfishness and pride, making even our righteousness in God's sight to be as filthy rags (Isa. 64:6). The literal translation of Isaiah 64:6 says that "our righteousness in God's sight is as a menstrual cloth." Why did God use such an analogy? A menstrual cloth is not filthy or evil, for menstruation is the normal, God-created function of a woman's body, a physical process which has a very meaningful purpose. God uses the analogy of a menstrual cloth, not as a synonym for evil or filth, but because a menstrual cloth is an indication that there is no new life in the woman's body. It reveals that she is not pregnant, that she is not carrying life inside of her. She is barren.

The Bible is not saying that we are totally filthy, vile, and evil. Rather, our problem is that we have no life inside us! We are totally barren. Dead. We are Lazarus.

Jesus prayed aloud and then "cried with a loud voice, 'Lazarus, come out' " (John 11:43, rsv). And he came out of death and the grave.

What a strange and frightening sight it must have been. When Lazarus walked out of the tomb, he was still wearing the grave clothes. He was "bound," and his face was covered with a napkin. Like a mummy, he struggled to walk. No doubt he made very little progress since he couldn't see where he was going and could only take tiny, uncertain steps. If he had to walk very far or tried to go very fast, he would surely stumble and fall. He was spiritually, mentally, and physically alive, but he was not getting anywhere very fast, if at all.

Then above the clamor and excitement caused by the miracle, Jesus shouted more life-giving instructions: "Unbind him, and let him go" (John 11:44, RSV). Cut off the grave clothes! Remove the blinders! Discard all the vestiges of death! Let him go! Let him move!

It is amazing how many have come to know life through Jesus Christ and yet go on dragging grave clothes with them. Frustrated followers of Christ refuse to allow the grave clothes to be removed and left beside the tomb of unbelief. They are like prisoners refusing to leave their death cells after the judge has granted them a full pardon and the prison doors stand open; liberated sons living as shackled slaves; travelers choosing dry sands of unrealized potential rather than the sparkling refreshment of an inviting oasis.

So many Christians, clinging to the grave clothes and refusing the coat of many colors, become a part of that large company who have only enough faith to be miserable. Like Lazarus they are alive but continue to stumble along, hindered by grave clothes.

Such people need help. All of us have fallen into this category at times, and when this happens, we need the help of others who can contribute to our liberation under the direction of Jesus Christ. The church performs this ministry for people. The church is to be the spiritual instrument whereby the "grave clothes" are removed, liberating *all* Christians to run and leap and shout, to wear colorful coats of many colors and go to parties as living testimonies to the life-giving power of Christ. Through this entirely new style of life we become witnesses for Jesus Christ and attract the world to him.

This is exactly what happened to Lazarus, and we are told about the results by an eyewitness in John 12. When Mary, Martha, and Lazarus came to know life through Christ, they attracted other people who also experienced a spiritual transformation. The Scripture says that many people came to see Lazarus whom Jesus had raised from the dead, and we are told that because of Lazarus's new life many others believed on Jesus (John 12:9–11).

Lazarus was a living testimony, incontrovertible evidence that Jesus Christ was the Son of God with power over death. The family and friends rejoiced and celebrated together at a party (John 12:2). Isn't that a tremendous picture of what the church is supposed to be? A party where people are celebrating their new life in Jesus Christ!

But this celebration caused a most unexpected reaction. Some people became very angry, and this is perplexing. Why did this miracle infuriate many influential leaders to the degree that they immediately began plotting the death of Jesus? Why did this miracle become, from a human standpoint, the catalyst that set off the chain reaction which culminated in the death of Jesus? Why is this miracle considered the greatest miracle in the ministry of Jesus?

If a man could raise another man from the dead, he would be the Son of God without any question, for any man who has the power over death and the grave and the power to give life is surely God's Son. This miracle is a picture, or a type, of what Christ has been doing for two thousand years— raising people from death "to walk in newness of life!" And this miracle is a picture of what Christ can do for *every* man: He raises men from death to life!

Since this miracle was such indisputable proof that Jesus Christ was the Son of God, the leaders of the land, who were—like most entrenched leadership—more concerned with the preservation of their position than with the resurrection of their fellow citizens, began plotting the death of Jesus. Though these men were evil, they were not stupid, for they also plotted the death of Lazarus. Wickedness may cause blindness, but like Samson, it is neither weak nor dumb. These men correctly reasoned that if they were to destroy Jesus they must also destroy this incontestable evidence. And Lazarus was a living testimony.

In the light of this incomparable story and all the truths it communicates, let me propose some new symbols of the Christian life. The Man on that donkey is a picture of Christ that has long been avoided by his followers. The same is true of the picture of the Christian life which we receive from the experience of Lazarus, his family, and friends.

Many people falsely picture a Christian as someone clothed in black, dragging along in a dull, drab existence and living a colorless, joyless life. He is frequently pictured as one primarily concerned with things he doesn't do, preoccupied with negatives, constantly subtracting from life, merely existing in a small, depressed, pinched, safe world. This is the picture, or the symbol, of Christianity that is too often presented to the world. In reality, such symbols picture death and the grave and are as far removed from what a Christian actually is as darkness is from light.

I propose that we allow the liberated Lazarus to be one of the rediscovered symbols of the Christian life. I believe it is obvious that the Lord intends for Lazarus to be recognized as the true picture of Christianity because of the prominent place this story has in the Bible and because of the tremendous results of his testimony.

Lazarus is the new picture of the new life. He was

raised from the dead, delivered from the confinement of a tomb, liberated from the grave clothes, and went to a party! He lived without the grave and without the *garbage* of the grave clothes. That's right, *garbage,* for garbage literally means "the garb of age," "old clothes," a covering, or clothing, which has been discarded because it is worn and old.

The Christian has had the "old garb" of grave clothes cut away and has been given new, bright, colorful, exciting clothes! His clothing is so colorful that people come to look at it. This new clothing is actually his new life which shows itself in the rainbow of color that brightens his face, his home, his work. To be a "witness" means to be *alive* in Christ, attracting people to him.

We should not be too surprised, although we are disappointed, that some people are resentful and envious. They were of Lazarus, and they will be of others. There will always be that mournful minority who resent a living witness, who resent life, color, new "garb." Just remember that the Lord doesn't stop the party because some refuse to attend.

This event is reminiscent of an incident in the Old Testament when Jacob, the loving father, gave his beloved son Joseph a "coat of many colors" (Gen. 37:3–4, KJV). Joseph's brothers were filled with such envy and jealousy that they tried to dispose of Joseph by selling him as a slave. They resented the beautiful and colorful verification of the father's love bestowed on Joseph.

Our loving heavenly Father has taken away the garbage of death and covered us with the colorful coat of eternal life. We are his sons! We are the people who wear rainbows! We look good! Having left death and all its garb-age in the grave, we, like Joseph, wear colorful coats of salvation, a gift from our loving Father.

God invites us to the party, to a life that sparkles with all the colors of the rainbow. He urges us to join the children of God, put on colorful coats of salvation, and feast and dance on our own vacated graves.

The
Empty
Perfume
Bottle

IN THE FRIGHTENING stillness the storm gathered for a final outburst of fury. Beyond the horizon the hurricanelike forces of death gained momentum.

Jesus had been teaching and preaching for about three years. Numberless lives had been changed: The blind had received their sight; the guilt-ridden had been delivered from their frustrations through the grace of forgiveness; astounding miracles of transformation had occurred.

But in spite of the joy and excitement, a sinister, hostile force was at work in the shadows, plotting extermination. Jesus walked quietly with his friends and said, "As you know, the Passover celebration begins in two days, and I shall be betrayed and crucified" (Matt. 26:2, LB). What a shattering, unbelievable statement! It was like hearing a knock on the door in the middle of the night. You open it to learn that one dear and close to you has died. Time stands still, and all you can hear is the throbbing of your own heart. Your world has crashed and burned.

At the very moment Jesus was making that terrifying statement to his friends, "the chief priest and other Jewish officials were meeting at the home of Caiaphas, the High Priest, to discuss ways of capturing Jesus quietly and killing him" (Matt. 26:3–4, LB). The atmosphere was filled with the kind of quivering quietness that prefaces a devastating storm. The most prominent religious figures of the day met in the home of the moral leader of all Judaism, plotting ways to capture and kill a carpenter from Nazareth whose only crime was advocating that men should "love God with all their heart, and their neighbor as themselves." I suppose the message of love has always sounded subversive to those who have made an idol of law and a graven image of ritualism.

Wickedness in high places is nothing new. Evil has always been rampant in our world, surfacing occasionally in a colossal explosion of iniquity to remind us that man lives in an Orwellian society where the only truth is slogans, the only duty is conformity, and the only morality is power.

Those first-century "law and order" advocates, like their successors, were anxious to perform their dastardly deed in such a way that the people would not know about it. With the cleverness that evil often produces, these "learned" men reasoned correctly that if the people heard of their plans during Passover there would probably be a riot.

I wonder who called the meeting "to order." Who made the motion to break the law in the name of the law? Who suggested committing murder in the name of righteousness? The decaying corpse of the "body" of religious legalism filled the room as it would ultimately fill the world with the rancid odor of unrealizable hopes.

The extent to which iniquity will go in the name of righteousness is amazing. Man's ability to baptize his sins, turning his vices into virtues, is still another proof of his indescribable depravity. It has always been true that the best corrupted inevitably becomes the worst.

Where was Jesus while all of this was taking place? What was he doing? Was he planning a counteraction? Was he gathering troops for a surprise attack? No, not at all. Of course he knew what

75

was happening, and none of it was unexpected. In the eye of this hurricane of hate he calmly walked to Bethany, three or four miles from the other meeting, and there went into the home of Simon the leper (Matt. 26:6).

Contrast the cast of characters at these two separate meetings. In one we see the respected religious leaders of the land—men who teach the Holy Scriptures, who lead others in the worship of God. These are holy men of law and learning; yet they meet secretly to plot the death of the only man whose entire life was totally devoted to helping others.

Jesus, his disciples, and friends met in the home of Simon the Leper. No doubt, Simon had been healed by Jesus. What a magnificent picture! A man whom Jesus had made a Christian now makes his home a church.

Some churches give a sadly different picture to the world, leaving the impression that they are spiritual supermen who have "arrived" rather than moral lepers who have been healed and who gather to thank Jesus for what he has done and is doing in their lives. When this pious impression is created, it is not surprising that people avoid such churches. Who can blame them? The lake, the ball game, or the bed is more attractive on Sunday morning than churches composed of sinners who think they are

76

saints rather than saints who know they are sinners.

Jesus' membership in the Church of Simon the Leper declares that every true, Bible-believing, Christ-honoring church in the world will be a home for the sick of soul. It will be a place of healing and hope for all who have given up and quit trying. The true church is composed entirely of lepers who have been healed by Jesus Christ and who spend their time inviting other moral cripples to come into a party of healing to enjoy the banquet and celebration of wholeness in Christ.

If this sounds strange or undignified, then in all likelihood you have never properly understood the actual condition of your own spiritual life. This is what we are: All of us have been infected with the leprosy of sin and unbelief. We are all moral lepers. If Jesus Christ has healed us with his grace, then we are Christians, but we are not Christians because we have cleansed ourselves. We are Christians because we confessed our corruption and he forgave us. We are made whole, not because we are worthy, but because he is worthy; not because we are deserving, but because he is divine; not because we are lovable, but because he is all loving. If you will see this truth, experience God's grace, and follow this Man, I invite you to join the party of healed lepers . . . join the church!

At Simon's home a most dramatic event occurred. As Jesus was eating his dinner, a woman entered the room with a bottle of extremely expensive perfume and, to the surprise of everyone, poured the perfume on Jesus. What a dramatic interruption! What a beautiful gesture! Surely everyone there was excited by this spontaneous gift of love and joined in the celebration and praise. It seems only natural that the woman's open adoration and devotion would have sparked similar feelings and expressions from the others present. But, surprising as it may seem, it didn't have that effect at all. Jesus' own disciples, of all people, were indignant and angry, a response even more surprising than the woman's gift. "What a waste of good money," they said. "Why, she could have sold it for a fortune and given it to the poor" (Matt. 26:8–9, LB). Using words that dripped with the sugar of feigned compassion they chilled the happy atmosphere with their judgmental pronouncement designed to make others feel guilty and thereby conceal their own proud, envious, joyless hearts.

But their attitude is not really astonishing when we reflect upon the reaction of most people to something happy, particularly when it relates to the Christian faith. Joy and vitality in our faith seem to be particularly upsetting to those who confuse

masochism with devotion, solemnity with spiritual-
ity, and who erroneously believe that God somehow
loves us more if we are sad and sick than if we are
happy and well. The first disciples tried to camouflage their real feelings with the pious veneer of supposed concern for others.

An embarrassed silence filled the room like a
gloomy cloud. Jesus knew what everyone was thinking, and he broke the tenseness with strong, reveal-
ing words: "Why are you criticizing her? For she has
done a good thing for me. You will always have the
poor among you, but you won't always have me.
She has poured this perfume on me to prepare my
body for burial. And she will always be remembered
for this deed. The story of what she has done will be
told throughout the whole world, wherever the Good
News is preached" (Matt. 26:10–13, LB). The disciples no doubt felt ashamed, and I imagine that
they quietly, one by one, got up and walked outside.

But one of the disciples couldn't stand the self-
disclosure. This kind of "gospel" was too devastating
to his ego. At that very moment Judas Iscariot, one
of the twelve apostles, realized he belonged in the
other meeting at the home of Caiaphas. If Jesus' disciples were going to be remembered for giving rather
than getting, for sacrifice rather than power, then
Judas wanted no part of it. He had had it. He left

immediately. Feeling out of place in the Church of Simon the Leper, Judas transferred his membership to the Church of Caiaphas the Pharisee.

Judas had seen countless lives changed. He was a man who had been blessed by the Man, one who had been privileged to live in the personal presence of the love of God; yet he "went to the chief priests, and asked, 'How much will you pay me to get Jesus into your hands?' And they gave him thirty silver coins. From that time on, Judas watched for an opportunity to betray Jesus to them" (Matt. 26:14–17, LB).

All of this seems so utterly fantastic that it is difficult to believe it happened at all. Yet it did, just as the Scripture described it, and the same sad story has been repeated thousands of times since. The basic plot remains unchanged, only the names of the people—Judas, the woman, the disciples, Caiaphas—change from day to day and place to place.

Jesus said that the story of this gift of spontaneous love would be told wherever the gospel is proclaimed, wherever the Good News is told. Why did he say that? Why did he place such a high evaluation upon this gift? Because this woman's deed symbolizes what happens to everyone who really hears the Good News. Jesus recognized in this dramatic incident the beautiful combination of ingredients that constitute genuine love—what love is and what love does. The gospel is a gospel of love, and one woman, touched by divine love, expressed her devotion in the most meaningful way she knew.

Jesus had already poured into her soul the priceless perfume of forgiveness, and her response to his matchless gift was to express her feelings of love with the loveliest gift she could secure. Suddenly, unexpectedly—interrupting the meal, upsetting the decorum of the moment—this woman spontaneously expressed her love for Jesus Christ by pouring expensive perfume over his head. Spontaneity is surely one of the most beautiful aspects of love. Those extremely rare moments when the unpredictable explosion of love's aroma fills a room, a house, a life, cannot be programmed and yet are as necessary as breathing.

The disciples' attitude was bad, but their evaluation was correct. Disciples, then and now, are often better at counting than at loving. It has been said that that gift represented enough money to feed at least five thousand people, an entire year's salary for a working person of that day. Our world cries for such uncalculating goodness to erupt out of the desert of materialism. How desperately the church, suffering with dullness and dustiness, needs to be touched again by the invigorating aroma of spontaneous love.

Of course, the church is only the combination of

all the people, feelings, hopes, and faith that constitute the fellowship. What we say about the church we are actually saying about ourselves, for we are the church. It is not a building we attend; the church is a body we share. If something is wrong with the church (and there is), something is wrong with you and with me.

In far too many churches the excitement of a new discovery has been slowly replaced by a dutiful adherence to boring ritual and routine. Consequently, there is more dust about us than dew. Because the natural and necessary effervescence of genuine faith has fizzled out, most of our "goodness" has become calculated and organized. Our giving is too sensible, our devotion too controlled, our service too predictable. The electronic calculator has become a more appropriate symbol of our faith than perfume bottles. As a result, our books are balanced, but our lives are not. The heart has gone out of our giving, partially because we keep at least one eye on the Internal Revenue Service instead of both eyes firmly fixed on external Christian service.

Most of us give in such small amounts. We keep "saving" ourselves as if we were being personally diminished rather than spiritually increased. Our giving is more like the delicate, occasional spray of an atomizer rather than the emptying of the entire contents of the perfume bottle. We hold back and conserve. The effect of our giving is short-lived; the aroma quickly wears off.

At Pentecost, because of their excitement, the disciples were accused of being intoxicated. We seldom hear that accusation today. It is sad when divine intoxication begins to wear off. Many people sing, but there is no music. They speak, but there is no sparkle. They work, but there is no wonder. They give, but there is no aroma.

We have become so agonizingly cautious about everything that we don't even move. "Look before you leap," we are told. So all we do is look, never leap. We are too careful. Our churches, denominations, and mission boards are prisoners of propriety. Seneca was correct: "Custom is king." Decorum is more in vogue than daring. It disturbs us to realize that if we really believed the gospel, if we really believed Christ is returning soon, if we really believed, we would explode with the kind of Spirit-directed recklessness and God-inspired intoxication that would begin to change the atmosphere of the entire world.

What is love like? It is spontaneous. It interrupts a meal. It doesn't wait for the proper moment, and it isn't concerned with acceptable procedures. It just explodes with instantaneous affection.

The timing of this gift was also significant. The woman was so filled with genuine love that she gave right then, right there, at that one sensitive moment. She was so filled with gratitude and emotion for the Man who had changed her life that it just happened—immediately!

There is a time to give bread and a time to give perfume, and it is not a question of one or the other. Jesus does not minimize the need to give bread by saying there will always be poor people around. He never said that we should give a bottle of Chanel when a loaf of Sunbeam is needed, for he gave bread himself. He supplied thousands by multiplying bread to feed the hungry. Jesus recognized that life without bread is impossible, and life without perfume is intolerable. Man cannot live at all without bread, and he cannot live at his best without perfume.

There is a time to pray, to play, to preach, to sing, to listen, to work, to worship, to weep, to rejoice. There is a gift for all seasons, and God will inspire us to give whatever gift is most needed at the moment.

"You men who are fathers," Jesus asked, "if your boy asks for bread, do you give him a stone? If he asks for fish, do you give him a snake?" (Luke 11: 11–12, LB). The answer is implied in the question. What is given is determined by the need. If we confront a poisonous snake, we would certainly rather have a stone than bread—at least for that moment. So the needs of the moment determine the nature of the gift, and the Holy Spirit can inspire us to be sensitive to the needs of others so that he can give to them, through us, that which is most needed.

When the Spirit of God impresses you that it is time to give, then give that which you feel is most needed at that moment.

A word of caution is in order. In all likelihood if we allow that inspired moment to escape us, the opportunity will be lost forever. Many times we have felt impressed to write a note or make a telephone call to someone expressing our love and appreciation, but we let something distract us, and we postpone our act of love. When that has happened, do we ever fulfill that moment of initial inspiration? Usually, if we do not act when impressed, we never act at all. Whenever God moves, move! Act! Go! Do! "For good deferred is evil indulged."

Extravagant, spontaneous, instantaneous love has another quality. It lasts. It has staying power. We often think of that which is effervescent as being transitory and temporary. We think of spontaneity as a kind of spiritual whipped cream, but this is not so. When I was a young man, my father would say as we sat down to the table, "This is a great meal;

it will really stick to your ribs." This is true when applied to the spiritual world as well. Spontaneous love is not a fluffy dressing; it is T-bone steak! It really sticks to your ribs.

Jesus said that the love and giving epitomized by this woman would be talked about forever. He was indicating that this kind of spontaneous, instantaneous giving of love has staying power. It will stick to the ribs of the world forever.

Dinner was finished; the guests had departed; and events moved inexorably toward the cross. Jesus died . . . arose . . . appeared! He lived! Then he commissioned his followers to declare the Good News everywhere! Many of them obeyed, and Christ began to change the entire world through the lives of these changed men and women who shared their faith.

A year goes by, ten years, one hundred years, a thousand! Two thousand years go by, and here we are today, reading and talking about what love did! As we mention this incident, we fulfill prophecy. We are doing exactly what Jesus said we would be doing —exclaiming about the power of spontaneous love. Truly he is the Son of God, and his "word will not pass away."

Civilizations die, governments collapse, buildings and businesses disappear, but divine, spontaneous love remains forever. When the pebble of love is unexpectedly dropped into the pool of placid, everyday, ordinary behavior, it causes waves.

The disciples said, "That perfume is worth a fortune, and the money could be given to the poor. Why are you wasting it?" For the most part the disciples were great people, and although it took some time, they finally caught on to who Jesus was and what he was all about. It took some of them longer than others, but the same is true with each of us. However, at this point, they had not yet "caught" the truth, nor had they been "caught" by it. They were still terribly judgmental and disgustingly pious in their attitudes. Like most of us they were good "second-guessers," good "grandstand quarterbacks."

Why did the disciples have such a violent, negative reaction? Relaxing, half-asleep with the drowsiness that a full stomach produces, they were unaware of or indifferent to the meeting going on at Caiaphas's house. From comfortable couches of satisfaction they found it easy to pass judgment on others. Did they really care that much about the poor? Or were they, like most of us, caring only for themselves? Like us they mistakenly thought they *were* good because they *felt* good. Filled with rich food they soothed their troubled consciences by voicing loud concerns for the hungry.

Since these men had previously been discussing

which of them was to be vice-president in the kingdom of God, it is apparent that they were much
more concerned with personal position than with
the plight of the poor. Therefore to defend a guilty
conscience they did what guilty men always do—
accuse others. The least painful thing to do in such
an unsettling moment is to make loud speeches and
blame other people. Such diversionary tactics are
nothing new. Adam and Eve were the first practition-
ers, and the disciples were not the last to employ
this deception.

One of the disciples' problems was that a *woman*
gave the gift and received the blessing and thanks of
the Lord. These men lived in a male-dominated society where women were not supposed to be doing
things like that. They belonged out in the kitchen,
cleaning up the house, carrying water, or caring for
the children. Suddenly a woman intruded into their
deliberations about the kingdom of God and inter-
rupted a lazy, after-dinner discussion with an extravagant, spontaneous gift of affection. They were
indignant (which really means guilty), and they
were also jealous (which means guilty, too). Jealousy and guilt combined to produce an outburst of
criticism. And isn't most criticism born from the unholy union of these two parents? These men were

ashamed because they had failed to express their love to Christ. To defend a defenseless position they lashed out at others who did love and who did express it. How typical and how convicting.

From honest self-examination we know that one of the first reactions of the guilty man is to blame others, to point a finger at someone else, to shift responsibility somewhere else, to divert attention to others. "Why didn't she give that money to the poor?" they exclaimed in pious indignation. Caring only for themselves, they defended a guilty conscience by accusing others.

This attitude of jealousy and guilt in *all* of them crystallized in *one* of them—Judas. How did Judas handle his guilt? He did what guilt always does when it can no longer stand the sight of itself; he exploded in an orgy of self-destruction. Unless the intolerable intensity of increasing guilt is released and relieved through the cleansing of confession and forgiveness, it will always self-destruct. Sometimes the process is sudden; most often it is a slow, day-by-day dying.

But guilt seldom vents its full fury exclusively on itself; it can be so blind that in its frenzy to protect itself, it lashes out wildly at the innocent. Judas did exactly that. In a pattern typical of all guilt, Judas attempted to destroy the love that revealed his hate, the light that revealed his darkness, the joy that revealed his misery, the life that revealed his death.

Judas sold his Lord for the price of a slave—thirty pieces of silver—only to find out too late that he was the slave he had sold. Struggling to find freedom from his guilt-ridden conscience, he went to the wrong priest—to Caiaphas instead of Christ. He returned the money to Caiaphas thinking he could buy deliverance from guilt when all the while Christ was dying to buy Judas's soul from the control of guilt and sin.

How many have made the same tragic mistake? How many, balancing in their minds right and wrong, fling down the right and choose the wrong, thinking it to be the way to freedom? The freedom they seek inevitably proves to be a delusion. When the mirage of temptation is lifted, we see sin as a barren desert, a desolate wilderness whose wastes are endless. Its waters are bitter and its shade is spiritual darkness. Its singing birds are but the bats and owls from the caves of doom; its murmuring breezes are but the hissings of fiery serpents. Its beauty is artificial; its promises are false; its guides are liars. Its reward is a terrible, lonely death, for "the wages of sin is death" (Rom. 6:23, KJV), and "the soul that sinneth, it shall die" (Ezek. 18:4, 20, KJV).

With whom do you identify in this story? With the religious crowd at the home of Caiaphas? With the disciples? With Judas? With the woman? One of the attitudes reflected in the people in this story dominates and controls our lives. We are most likely a mixture of all of these, but one attitude prevails, one characteristic is dominant. Which is it?

If what we see of ourselves as we look into the mirror of this story disturbs us, then we can change. With the transforming touch of the loving Christ, everyone of us can give the perfume of our lives to Christ. We can pour it out onto a tired, dreary world. And when our lives are poured out onto others, we will find that we have joined that growing number of aromatic people whose lives embody another of the new Christian symbols—empty perfume bottles.

Throw
Your
Life
Away

ARE YOU TRYING to lose weight? Most people at one time or another have attempted to get rid of a few pounds. Not long ago a man said to my friend, "You've lost some weight haven't you?" My friend replied, "Yes, I've lost thousands of pounds the last few years—but the same ones. I just keep gaining them back."

Everyone is conscious of his or her size, and this is normal. There are some things about my size for which I am responsible, but there are some things for which I am not responsible. For example, I cannot determine my height. As much as I might like to be six feet six, I cannot make myself that tall. Although I cannot control my height, I can, if I will, control my weight. I cannot select the color of my eyes, but I can decide what I will see. The shape of my ears is beyond my control; what I decide to hear is not.

Most likely we have all seen some of those "Before and After" advertisements. Recently I saw one that stated, "After losing one hundred pounds, I weigh less now than when I was twenty-two years old." Pictured in the advertisement was a woman, minus the one hundred pounds. There was no doubt about it—there was a big improvement. The woman continued: "Now that I am fifty-two years old, I am down to one hundred thirty-four pounds, and I feel spry as a spring chicken." I suppose that means she feels good! She also stated that she had changed the color of her hair. That too is all very fine and good. Considering the limitations most of us have, I firmly believe that if any improvement in our appearance encourages our attitude about ourselves, then we ought to try to make that improvement. Personally I am not as much concerned about my hair turning gray as I am about its turning loose, and it seems to be doing some of both!

We are able to take a physical picture of ourselves and get some idea about the way we look, but it is impossible for us to photograph our soul. What size would my soul be if it were possible to photograph it? Would it be large or small? Big or little?

With or without an actual photograph, we have at last uncovered one area in life where all of us need to gain some weight. Our souls need to grow, and our spirits should be constantly increasing in size. In this part of life it is not only permissible, but marvelously advantageous, to be large. We can gain as much as we like, and the results are good and healthy. Another encouraging fact is that the food necessary for this growth is easily found and thoroughly prepared. It *is* possible to "feed" our souls so that they will grow and grow and grow!

This discussion about size reminds me of a story in the Bible about a little man and the problems he faced because of his size.

As Jesus was passing through Jericho, a man named Zacchaeus, one of the most influential Jews in the Roman tax collecting business (and, of course, a very rich man), tried to get a look at Jesus, but he was too short to see over the crowds. So he ran ahead and climbed into a sycamore tree beside the road, to watch from there.

When Jesus came by he looked up at Zacchaeus and called him by name! "Zacchaeus!" he said. "Quick! Come down! For I am going to be a guest in your home today!"

Zacchaeus hurriedly climbed down and took

Jesus to his house in great excitement and joy.

But the crowds were displeased. "He has gone to be the guest of a notorious sinner," they grumbled.

Meanwhile, Zacchaeus stood before the Lord and said, "Sir, from now on I will give half my wealth to the poor, and if I find I have overcharged anyone on his taxes, I will penalize myself by giving him back four times as much!"

Jesus told him, "This shows that salvation has come into this home today. This man was one of the lost sons of Abraham, and I, the Messiah, have come to search for him and to save such souls as his" (Luke 19:1-10, LB).

Here is a biblical "Before and After" picture. "Before," Zacchaeus was a little, cheating, conniving, contemptuous man who, because he hated himself, hated everyone else. His attitude is not too surprising. All of us project onto others the feelings that we have about ourselves. We nearly always do unto others what we are doing unto ourselves.

Zacchaeus, a Jew, had sold out to the Roman invaders and had become a tax collector which, as far as the Jews were concerned, was about the worst thing any man could do. Consequently, he was considered a traitor by his fellow countrymen. Externally or internally you cannot get a much smaller picture of a man's soul than the one you get of Zacchaeus. He was a miniature man.

From the story we get the impression that people were somehow *always* getting in his way, and when they did, Zacchaeus found some way to step on them, over them, or around them. Apparently he looked upon others as adversaries, and whether they actually were or not was unimportant; because he looked upon people as enemies, that's what they became. The comedian Flip Wilson has an amusing saying that is also a fact of life: "What you see is what you get." He uses the statement as a clever bit of humor, but the truth it conveys is not a joke.

What we see *is* what we get because we see what we look for. This attitude can be carried to such an extreme that sometimes we look for something so intently that we see it even if it is *not* there. Concentration and prejudice can combine to make a mountain out of almost any molehill. "To the pure all things are pure," not because impurity is not present, but because it is just not dwelt upon, not stared at constantly. What you see is what you get, and what you get will in time get you. The person I become is determined by what I choose to see.

THROW AWAY THE GARBAGE

This story also illustrates that it *is* possible for the crowd to get in the way of a conscientious seeker after truth. Although the previous practices of Zacchaeus understandably made the crowd suspect his motives, no one, particularly a crowd, can accurately determine a man's deepest motives. It is natural for people to react on the basis of one's previous performance, and the previous performance of Zacchaeus had certainly not endeared him to the people of Jericho. Because another's motives are unknown, or unexpressed, it is possible for the crowd to obstruct the way of a very sincere and earnest seeker after the Lord. The crowd that may sometimes impede rather than inspire the seeking Zacchaeuses of the world just *may* be the crowd in the church. Churches which see themselves as a crowd of saints rather than a family of sinners are particularly susceptible to this destructive disease, and the disease is highly contagious.

In the Bible the word *sin* literally means to "miss the mark." It doesn't necessarily mean that the person intentionally tries to miss the target; it doesn't mean that he shoots in the opposite direction; it means that he shoots toward the target, but he misses the bull's-eye. In this sense we, like Zacchaeus, are all sinners. Zacchaeus was like the crippled man sitting at the gate of the Temple begging for money when Peter and John passed by and said to him, "We don't have any money, but in the name of Jesus Christ, stand up and walk." What the man wanted was money, but what he needed was legs! Often our wants are not our needs. Zacchaeus needed forgiveness; he needed to be reconciled to God, to his family, and to his neighbors, but what he wanted was money. And money he had! He had what he wanted but not what he needed.

In many ways Zacchaeus is modern man's ideal. He had won! How he played the game made no difference; he had won, and that was all that counted. Zacchaeus was resented by his contemporaries, but their resentment was not because he had sold out, for they had done—or would have done—the same thing. Zacchaeus was disliked because he had made betrayal into such a profitable business. It was not his betrayal of principle that created the resentment of his fellow citizens nearly so much as his ability to make the vocation of a traitor so financially lucrative. If anyone thinks we are describing actions and attitudes out of the dusty pages of history, he need only look at the dirty transcripts of Richard Nixon's tapes to see the same forces at work. The *only* thing that counted was winning; the *only* sin was to lose. This was the dominant motive in Zacchaeus, in Nixon, in millions of others less famous in the eye of the public but no less infamous in the eye of God. Sin is always dangerous, but it is never so fatal as when it enjoys material success.

It was no tragedy that Zacchaeus was physically small, for he had no control over that. The tragedy was that Zacchaeus had allowed an external condition to become an internalized attitude. Zacchaeus mistakenly thought that size and worth were the same, that quality and quantity were synonymous. He wasn't the first, and unfortunately won't be the last, to make that mistake. Zacchaeus was physically small but became spiritually little. Seeing himself as little, he lived down to his expectations. Trying to gain the whole world, he shriveled his own soul. Zacchaeus attempted to make himself big by making everyone else small; he elevated himself by suppressing others; he put himself up by putting everyone else down. A circumstance became a problem that became a sickness that became a sin.

This chain reaction of spiritual self-destruction made Zacchaeus susceptible to becoming a tax collector in the first place. He discovered that by this method he could gain power over other people; since he couldn't control himself, he would control others as a substitute. Zacchaeus created in the response of others the attitude he had toward himself, and because he so disliked himself, others disliked him. As a result of this sick procedure, Zacchaeus gained a degree of satisfaction from their hatred. Their hostility at least confirmed his existence. The hatred of others, although unpleasant, affirmed his presence on the planet. Spiritually little men are willing to sacrifice anything to prove they at least exist.

Some would analyze Zacchaeus's problem as low self-esteem. This evaluation may be true, but it is only another way of stating that Zacchaeus was the type of man who had never seen himself as a sinner extremely valuable because he is personally loved by the eternal God. What is described as low self-esteem is often the result of sin that is unconfessed because the love of God is unrecognized. It is impossible to dislike or belittle that which God loves and for which he gave his life. Zacchaeus, like countless others, was lost because he had misplaced his love, his confidence, and his faith. Anyone who has lost all of that is not going to think much of himself.

The soul of Zacchaeus had shriveled until he had become a midget-spirited man, vainly attempting to solve his problem in the wrong way, using others for his own selfish purposes. Zacchaeus had slashed his spiritual wrists and was slowly and surely dying. Unable to find himself, and unconcerned about others, Zacchaeus was lost.

In the Bible the word *lost* does not only mean

eternal damnation, it also means "misplaced." It means to be out of relationship. Zacchaeus was lost, misplaced, out of relationship to God and to others. He would eventually be ultimately lost in eternity, but he was presently lost in Jericho. He had misplaced his dreams, his goals, his faith, his self-evaluation. With all that money and power, Zacchaeus was lost.

We can see what was happening to Zacchaeus, but what are you and I doing with our dreams and hopes? In whom are they placed? In what or in whom do we trust? Every man must trust someone or something. In whom or in what have we placed our faith? Is it possible that we, like Zacchaeus, have misplaced our dreams and hopes? The misplacement of one's dreams and hopes and faith is what it means to be "lost," and the consequences are tragic now, today, in this life. The ultimate result of such misplacement is compounded and finalized in eternity.

Like all of us, Zacchaeus was lost. Everyone is lost, for we have all misplaced our faith. Having put our faith in things, it is natural to feel that the more things we accumulate, the more security we will have, the more "saved" we will be. Like Zacchaeus, we try to top everyone else. We climb over people in our quest for self-realization and actualization, and in the process we lose our souls, our friends, and our self-respect. We find ourselves up a tree—lonely, isolated, afraid, frantically looking for someone or something to give our accumulation of things some lasting meaning. In the midst of our anguish, Jesus comes to the base of our "ego-tree" and says, "Come down."

That was the one thing Zacchaeus didn't want to do, for "down" was where he had always been. He had spent years climbing over the lives and feelings of others in his frantic attempt to prove he was "Mr. Big." Suddenly, the fantastic carpenter, the builder of men, shattered all his hollow hopes with the humbling words, "Come down." The thoughts of these two are not recorded in the Bible, but I believe that, in the brief silence that followed, Jesus and Zacchaeus carried on a dramatic nonverbal conversation.

Zacchaeus had not climbed that tree by accident, by some twist of fate. No casual occurrence had placed Zacchaeus at the right place, at the right time to meet Jesus. God had planned that encounter from the beginning of time. Christ came to Jericho, attracted Zacchaeus, called him by name, and invited him down out of the tree. From the beginning the initiative of Christ prompted Zacchaeus's desire to see Jesus at all.

Even though Zacchaeus was not consciously aware of the fact, Jesus went to Jericho to meet Zacchaeus just as he has come to this very moment in your life and experience to meet you. He has been looking forward to this meeting since the first day of creation; it is no accident that you are reading these words at this second and that God's Holy Spirit is attracting you to Christ now. Exactly like Zacchaeus, Jesus has come to the place in your life to meet you now.

Each of us can experience what David described: "O Lord, you have examined my heart and know everything about me. You know when I sit or stand. When far away you know my every thought. You chart the path ahead of me, and tell me where to stop and rest. Every moment, you know where I am. You know what I am going to say before I even say it. You both precede and follow me, and place your hand of blessing on my head" (Ps. 139:1–5, LB).

The remarkable imagination of Jesus is revealed in the manner in which he used some physical circumstances to attract Zacchaeus. This does not alter the fact that God took the initiative in the experience of Zacchaeus—just as he does with everyone else—it only means that God can and does use every possible means to attract us to himself.

106

The loving initiative of a seeking Savior utilizes human instrumentalities. No doubt one of these was Jesus' reputation which had preceded him to Jericho. The word had gotten around that Jesus was a remarkable, unusual man. Some were saying that he even performed miracles and that he taught as no other man ever taught. A growing number of people were convinced that he was the Messiah!

The particulars may change, but the principle remains: Jericho becomes Jakarta, Bethlehem becomes Birmingham, but the reputation of Jesus still reaches out to attract the unattractive, invite the rejected, befriend the friendless. This very moment the Holy Spirit of God is using countless human channels to spread the reputation of Jesus throughout the entire world so as to attract the world to him. God takes this initiative and utilizes human instrumentality because he loves the world, and love *always* pursues the beloved! Divine love inspires the action, creates the attraction, and comes "to the place" to *fulfill* every expectation.

God used another human agency to attract Zacchaeus—the testimony of Matthew. Zacchaeus and Matthew probably knew each other, for Matthew was also a tax collector before he became a follower of the Lord. I doubt that the hated tax collectors, like Matthew and Zacchaeus, had many friends other than those engaged in the same detested business. They certainly would not have won any popularity contests and would therefore find their few acquaintances among those who were "birds of the same feather." If they were at all like modern Americans, they probably had an organization entitled AOHTC—"Association of Hated Tax Collectors." In all likelihood they attended an occasional "convention."

Suddenly, Matthew was converted to Christ! He was drastically and dramatically changed. Because he was so happy and because he wanted everyone who knew him or knew about him to hear the Good News, he gave a coming-out party. Matthew was coming out of his old life into the new and wonderful life which Christ had given him. Zacchaeus probably attended that party and heard Matthew share with everyone what Christ had done to give him the life which he had long sought in the wrong places. The testimony of Matthew, utilized by the Holy Spirit of God, could have become another human instrument to attract Zacchaeus to Christ and to convict him of his need.

The loving initiative of the Spirit of God, having first attracted Zacchaeus through the reputation of Jesus, added the powerful magnet of a man's per-

sonal account of Jesus' ability to give love and forgiveness.

The mind and heart of Zacchaeus is now recep-
tive to a personal encounter. He is at least curious
enough to want to see Jesus when he comes to town;
so he leaves the tax office on his lunch hour to go
see the Man. Unable to get close because of the huge
crowd, he climbs a tree and waits. Curiosity may
have killed the cat, but it is about to save a man.
We can never count the times the Holy Spirit has
used curiosity to encourage people to open the door
of their lives from the inside. Circumstances knock;
curiosity opens; Christ enters!

Zacchaeus is up in the tree. Christ and his crowd
come walking along the street. Just beneath the tree,
Christ stops. He has "come to the place." He looks
up and calls Zacchaeus by name. The impact on
Zacchaeus is explosive. He nearly falls out of the
tree. "He knows me," Zacchaeus shouts inside his
mind. "He knows my name!" And the crowd begins
to stir in a flurry of excited conversation as the whole
scene is suddenly charged with the electricity of the
unexpected.

Jesus knew Zacchaeus. He knew all about him just
as he knows all about all of us. He knows everything, a fact that is both embarrassing and encouraging. We can't believe anyone would want us

or like us knowing what we are really like inside our minds. Yet the one person in all the world who really knows us really wants us to be his friend.

Jesus knew what kind of man Zacchaeus was. He knew how crooked he had been in all of his business dealings and personal practices. He knew about Zacchaeus's low self-image, his hostilities, his jealousies, his littleness, his sin; yet in spite of all that Zacchaeus was and had been, Christ invited him to come down and to go have lunch. Jericho would never forget that scene; everyone who witnessed it would go on talking about it for years and years— nearly two thousand of them to be exact.

Zacchaeus half falls, half climbs down from the tree, and he and Jesus start walking toward his house. By the time they arrive, the few people in Jericho who had not been around the tree had heard the word and had joined the crowd gathering around the house. Everybody in town was standing around outside discussing what could possibly happen next.

We are not told the details of the conversation or any words Jesus may have spoken. The first words recorded are those of Zacchaeus who stands to his feet and makes a startling announcement: "Sir, from now on I will give half of my wealth to the poor, and if I find I have overcharged anyone on his taxes,

I will penalize myself by giving him back four times as much!"

Such an unexpected verbal explosion no doubt had a tremendous impact on everyone. The Scriptures only relate the response of Jesus; can you even begin to imagine the reaction of the crowd, those people who knew and hated Zacchaeus, who had been cheated out of their money by him? Excitement spread like wildfire throughout Jericho.

Since we are not told what Jesus said privately to Zacchaeus, we can only speculate. However from what the Bible does tell us, we are impressed that it was not Jesus who talked to Zacchaeus about Zacchaeus's sins; Zacchaeus spoke about his own sins. The quiet power of the Light of the World confronts the darkness of sin and causes that sin to reveal itself. In the presence of light, darkness always dies.

The nature of Zacchaeus's Christ-inspired confession was very specific. He did not just say "I'm sorry," but he demonstrated the genuineness of his commitment to Christ both by giving his money to the poor and by returning money plus interest to those from whom he had illegally taken it. Zacchaeus really "put his money where his mouth was."

This kind of spontaneous, objective, overt, follow-through, this "doing" and not just "saying," is described in the Bible as restitution. Because it is so personally painful, most of us have ignored restitution. It is so much easier to talk than to walk. Restitution is painful to our pride and maybe, like Zacchaeus, painful even to our pocketbooks. Christianity can get very costly in many ways when it is taken seriously. The Bible unmistakably teaches restitution, and genuine Christianity practices it.

How does this story relate to us? Like Zacchaeus, once Jesus Christ has approached us through a variety of people and circumstances, we respond to his personal invitation to come. We get off the high horse of our own pride and, ignoring the comments of others, begin to walk with him. It is all so very new and unpredictable, yet we recognize deep inside our lives that something is different. We are surprised and elated and a little afraid.

In the light created by the presence of this Man, we begin to see ourselves in an entirely new way. For the first time ever, we see ourselves as we *really* are. Stripped of all the external symbols of material success which we have unsuccessfully attempted to use to show the world that we have it made, a whole new way of "seeing" is created. We see Christ as love and light. We see ourselves and cry, "Lord, be merciful to me, a sinner." We see others and their needs and we start giving ourselves and our property. The entire meaning and purpose of life begins to dawn upon us, and for the first time we really begin to grow into men and women who are "full of grace and truth." We begin to gain the kind of weight we need to "grow in grace and in the knowledge of the Lord Jesus."

Lloyd Douglas stated it beautifully: " 'Zacchaeus,' said the Carpenter gently, 'what did you see that made you desire this peace?' 'Good Master, I saw, mirrored in your eyes the face of the Zacchaeus I was meant to be.' "

Do you feel you are the man or woman you were meant to be? Are you living the way you were meant to live? Are you doing what God created you to do? If not, then see mirrored in the eyes of Jesus the face of the man or woman you were meant to be. Realize that Christ can make you into that kind of man or woman if you will allow him. He will restore your life to all its proper relationships—to himself, to yourself, to your family, and to the world around you.

Jesus said, "If anyone hears me calling him and opens the door, I will come in and fellowship with him and he with me" (Rev. 3:20, LB).

Christ has been calling us through a thousand voices—friends, circumstances, his Word. If we will only open the door to let him in, all of life for now and eternity will be different. For the first time *ever*, we can look good, smell good, and be good!

The party begins; the banquet is served; the fun-feast starts! What a moment! We wear the bright, colorful clothes of salvation given us by our Father to replace the old grave clothes of sin—the garbage of death.

We get together wearing our new garb of grace, and because of the wonder and excitement of it all, we start pouring the intoxicating perfume of hope upon one another. The beautiful aroma of love begins to fill the earth! If we've wronged anyone, we make it right; when we see needs, we meet them; when we hear cries, we answer them; when we see tears, we dry them. We give and give and give.

When Michael, Stephen, and I walked out of that drugstore many years ago carrying our Mother's Day gifts of "Reckless Pink," "Intoxication," and the "Ten Commandments," we did not have the faintest idea that we were carrying in our hands the kind of living symbols that would so accurately express the Good News of Jesus Christ. How could lipstick, perfume, and a charm bracelet ever represent the gospel? Well, they did, and they do.

"Reckless Pink," "Intoxication," and the "Ten Commandments"! Look good! Smell good! Be good!

And that is good, for it is Godlike.